BASIC DOG TRAINING
KW-022

Contents

Overleaf: The well-trained dog is a joy to its master. **Title page:** The "Sit" command is one of the most basic commands in dog training.

Photography: Maria DiBenedetto, Ian Dunbar, Isabelle Francais, Larry Freas, Manolo Guevara, Barbara Lockwood, Vincent Serbin, Sally Anne Thompson. (Photos on pages 22, 30, and 31 are from Lew Burke's Dog Training.)

The portrayal of canine pet products in this book is for general instructive value only; the appearance of such products does not necessarily constitute an endorsement by the author, the publisher, or the owners of the dogs portrayed in this book.

BASIC DOG TRAINING
MILLER WATSON

Above: *The German Shepherd Dog, long a very popular breed, can be trained in many different capacities.* **Facing page:** *The Basset Hound (top left) may appear slow, but he is an eager learner of new commands. The Wirehaired Fox Terrier (top right) and long-haired Dachshunds (below) are equally adept at learning quickly, as they are bright breeds.*

The very first thing a dog must learn is to be clean in the house. Before explaining the best methods of teaching a puppy this elementary duty, I must first emphasize that in training a dog a little patience is worth more than a lot of beating. This is the first thing a dog owner must learn if he hopes to be successful in training his canine friend.

Some dogs are somewhat high strung and nervous, and hitting them only makes them upset. The most intelligent and best trained dogs I have ever seen have never been smacked or whipped. Admittedly there are stubborn dogs, just as there are stubborn people, and it may prove necessary, *after every other method has failed,* to administer a sharp smack to a pup that is determined to resist authority.

Before you ever smack a dog, however, make quite sure that the animal really understands what you want it to do. The best way of making sure is to withhold the smack and explain again.

A young puppy, just like a human baby, is bound to urinate very frequently. Nobody would think of smacking a baby because it wets its diapers, and nobody should think of smacking a puppy because it wets the floor.

To begin with, you must expect the puppy to make mistakes sometimes, but the best method of teaching is by taking the little animal out frequently.

When the pup is still very young it is advisable to take it outside every hour. When it "does its duty" outside, it should be petted and encouraged. When, by mistake, it soils the floor, the pup's nose should be held near the spot while a *verbal* scolding takes place. The dog very soon learns to know when its owner's voice indicates displeasure.

Having pointed out the fault, on no account speak again of the subject. Dogs hate "nagging." Neither should the scolding be too prolonged nor too severe. I have seen pups

Facing page: The Siberian Husky is known for its steadfast devotion and adaptability to all sorts of living conditions.

This pair of well-mannered Dachshunds, representing the Hound group, will sit at attention when ordered to do so. If your dog is taught with patience and ample rewards when he performs well, you should have no trouble in the future with disciplinary problems.

Representatives from five of the six dog groups. Top left: Affenpinscher; top right: Wirehaired Fox Terrier; middle left: Labrador Retriever; middle right: Harlequin Great Dane; right: Bulldog.

repeat the offense through sheer fright.

I can hear someone say, "Oh, but I tried that method and it didn't work. The pup just went on soiling the floor!" Most people who find that the pup is taking a long time to learn have not taken the dog out frequently.

As I said, the pup should be taken out every hour at first, even if it is only for a few minutes. Gradually the intervals between the outings can be increased as the animal's ability to control itself increases. If this is done, the number of "mistakes" in the house will be very few.

Some dogs learn quicker than others, and some breeds "train" much more quickly than others. Chows, for instance, are often quite housebroken at

It is important that you start a housebreaking training program for your puppy as soon as he arrives in your home.

The Shih Tzu is an active, lively dog that takes well to training sessions.

three months old and even younger. Compare this with a human baby and you will be duly grateful. In any case, whatever the breed, a pup should have learned to be clean in the house by the time it is five months old. By this I mean that it will be completely clean in the house, but much earlier than this it will have learned to ask out.

Simultaneously with housebreaking, a pup must be taught something else. And it is something which is unfortunately disregarded by many dog owners. A dog must learn to be clean outside as well as in the house. *It is an unpardonable thing that a dog owner should allow his dog to soil the pavements.*

Complaints are becoming more and more frequent about this nuisance, and even the

Above: The alertness of puppies, readily apparent in this trio of a Dalmatian, an Irish Setter, and a Shetland Sheepdog, is an important factor in training capabilities. *Facing page:* An inquisitive Beagle puppy (top left). Older dogs, such as this adult Bloodhound (top right) and this adult Dalmatian (bottom) can also learn new commands if taught with patience.

most fanatical dog-lover must admit that there is some reason for complaint. Dog owners who allow their dogs to get this dirty habit are doing an ill turn to all dog-lovers. And soon as they get out, and if they are taken to the gutter immediately they will soon learn that they must go there. It is hardly necessary to add that the puppy should be kept

If puppies receive proper amounts of affection and discipline, they will grow up to be happy and well-adjusted.

there is no excuse for the offense, because it is just as easy to "street-train" a dog as to "house-train" it.

When a puppy is taken out it should be on the lead, and it should be taken to the gutter. Most puppies will urinate as in the gutter for "both duties."

Now let us consider the "difficult" pup. It is true that some puppies, either because they are stubborn, or because they are unable to understand, take a long time to learn. In the first case, that is, when the

This Siberian Husky has been trained for weight-pulling. Taking a cartload of children for a ride will provide practice for a real weight-pulling competition.

puppy is stubborn, it may be necessary to adopt stronger methods.

A good way of punishing a stubborn pup is to smack it on the rear end with a folded newspaper. This does not hurt the dog, but it makes a good loud bang. If a puppy persists in soiling the floor this treatment may be adopted, *but never if the dog is of nervous disposition.* It is very seldom that a dog proves stubborn in this respect, and, in fact, most dogs are eager to please their masters. In the case of a dog that does not understand, patience is the wonder worker.

Facing page: This Shetland Sheepdog sits proudly at attention, displaying its mastery of obedience commands. **Right and bottom:** The Pembroke Welsh Corgi and Shih Tzu, both small breeds, do not usually present much of an obedience problem.

The dog's mistakes must be pointed out *in every case,* but when it does the right thing (outside) praise must be generous and prolonged. The best phrase to use when scolding is "bad dog" and for praising, "good dog." Always keep to the same phrase and the animal will finally come to understand it. Do not expect your dog to have a big vocabulary. It will never be able to distinguish between "bad" and "naughty." Use one word or another *always.*

Certain sounds seem to express disapproval to the doggy ear, and one of the best is "ach" (pronounced as by Germans or Scots). If you say "Ach, bad dog!" to any dog it will know you are displeased. People who have difficulty in pronouncing the guttural "ch" may use "ah-tut" or even "tut-tut." All these sounds mean disapproval to a dog.

Now a few "don'ts" about housebreaking:

Don't deprive your dog of water, or reduce its water ration, in the hope that it will urinate less. Pups require a lot of water, and it is definitely cruel to deprive them of it. It has been proven that dogs that have water always at their disposition thrive better than those that have to ask for a drink.

Don't smack your dog with your hand or hit it on the head. Never smack a dog at all unless it is absolutely necessary, but if you must do it, do it with a rolled or folded newspaper. A dog distrusts the hand that smacks it.

Don't rub your dog's nose where it has soiled. It is a filthy and useless punishment. Make the pup smell the place and then take it outside.

Don't treat the pavement as outside. Treat it as part of your or somebody else's house. Keep it clean.

Facing page: The Golden Retriever, with its eager and self-confident personality, is a good candidate for training. Because of their hunting capabilities, members of this breed derive much satisfaction from retrieving objects for you—and receiving your praise.

Learning to control your dog while on lead in the street is essential, particularly with a powerful breed such as the Doberman Pinscher. It is something that must be learned at a very young age.

At first, the dog may not like the taut pull of the lead, and he may try, even playfully, to bite at it.

Finally, the dog is subdued successfully. With time, he will look forward to such exercise excursions and not mind the lead at all. Photo series is of professional dog trainer Lew Burke.

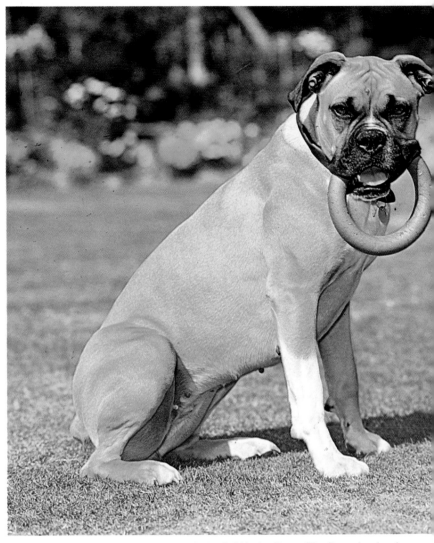

Resting during an exercise excursion in the field is the Boxer. The Boxer is a hardy dog who enjoys vigorous play and exercise. Training can be a part of your dog's daily exercise regimen. Take your pet to a large field, where you are certain that he cannot run loose into traffic or in the vicinity of other dogs. Toss an object to him, allowing him to catch it and return it to you.

Teaching Basic Obedience

Right from the very beginning a dog must learn to obey its master or mistress, and the first part of this is to come when called.

A puppy will learn to recognize its name very soon, and the first lesson in "calling" should be at a meal time. The puppy's food should be put in a dish and shown to the dog from a little distance. While showing the dish call the dog's name in an encouraging tone. This first lesson is easy and the pup never fails to understand the appeal of food. This gives the key to the whole business of teaching obedience. Make it a pleasure to obey and the dog will obey every time.

Pups are very fond of playing with an old toy or a ball, and this facilitates further lessons. Hold up the object and wave it about as you call the dog's name. The puppy sees the chance of a game and comes quickly. Always make a point of doing something to please the animal when it comes to you, and you will soon find that your dog will run to you every time it is called. The reward may sometimes be only a pat on the head, but even this little thing is appreciated by a dog.

When taking the puppy out, do not pick it up or fetch it to the door. Stand near the door and call. The pup, which is only too pleased to go outside and explore, will come running, and should be greeted with: "Good dog, out for a walk!" or some such phrase. Little sentences of this kind soon have a definite meaning to a dog, but the same expression should always be used for the same purpose. Avoid confusing the dog's mind by saying: "Come out, pup," one time, and "Out for a walk" another. Always use the same words, at least, while the dog is young.

Never tell your dog a lie. Do not call it saying "out for a walk" when you have no intention of taking it out and merely want the dog to come. If you do this the animal begins to doubt the meaning of the words and you will have great difficulty in teaching anything.

Facing page: This Beagle is demonstrating its mastery of the "Beg" command. When your dog performs as skillfully as this, always remember to praise it with kind words and a pat on the head.

The Cairn Terrier (left) and Longhaired Chihuahua (below) will require different training programs. The Cairn is feisty, true to his terrier heritage, and will require a firm hand lest he become snappy or irritable. The Chihuahua, on the other hand, is a tiny, delicate dog who will require less in the way of disciplining. **Facing page:** A mixed breed needs just as much training as any purebred dog, if he is to be well-behaved.

The dog must learn to have regular habits in the house. Its bed should be kept in the same place, and it should know where to find its water dish. If you should happen to

Ample opportunity for socialization with its littermates is important to a puppy's development.

have a fireplace, from its youngest days your dog must learn to keep back from the fire. Dogs that are allowed to sit in front of the fire frequently ruin their eyes, and in any case they are liable to catch colds.

If you, yourself, are sitting near the fire, make the puppy sit down at your side, but as far back from the fire as possible. When the dog goes near the fire (as it will do), draw it back gently but firmly and say: "Back from the fire!" You may have to repeat this warning many times before the dog finally understands, but ultimately you will be successful.

Some people prefer to teach their dogs to lie down in a corner well removed from the fire, and there is no doubt that their coats benefit from this. It is an easily taught habit, all that is necessary being to carry the pup into the corner whenever it gets sleepy. Most people, however, prefer to have their pets sitting beside them, and there is no harm done as long as they are not allowed to "toast their noses."

Pups must be taught not to chew furniture, and the best way is prevention rather than cure. If the pup is always supplied with a safe chew object such as a Nylabone®, it will not think of chewing such things as furniture. There are a great variety of Nylabone® products available. These hard-nylon therapeutic devices channel doggie tension and chewing frustration into constructive rather than destructive behavior.

If the puppy insists on chewing on forbidden objects, you might cure his bad habit by putting mustard on the object in question (without, of course, letting the puppy see you do so). I have found this generally quite sufficient, although I remember one dog that had a rather strong palate and seemed to enjoy the mustard. I mixed a little cayenne pepper with the mustard, however, and found this definitely stopped the chewing.

If your puppy destroys any small object, an effective punishment is the following. Point to the object and say: "Bad dog!" Then, scolding all the while, tie the object to its collar (or around its neck), in such a way that it hangs down in front of its legs. Leave this on for an hour or so.

Training your pet to retrieve can begin when the animal is twelve weeks of age.

A useful thing that can be taught in the house is to make the dog remain in a given spot. Sit the puppy somewhere, and holding up a pointed finger say: "Stay!" Then back slowly

An excellent training tool is the choke collar, which tightens as the dog pulls on the lead, teaching him to restrain himself. Shown is the method of correctly applying the collar.

An older child who can be patient with his dog and not tease him may train him to perform a number of obedience commands. This boy is teaching his pet the "Heel" and "Stay" commands.

away, keeping your finger up. After a few steps the puppy will usually follow you, but put it back in the place and repeat the command. Whenever the puppy waits for a very short time, return to it and praise it. The distance can gradually be increased, but the lesson should never be too long. Puppies soon get tired of a "game," and once tired it is hard to get them to try again.

I was once teaching a spaniel to "sit," and I had reached the stage where the dog would wait even after I was out of its sight. One day I told it to wait with a suitcase and went into another room, meaning to return a few minutes later. Something else got my attention, however, and it was two hours later when I remembered the dog. The obliging animal was still sitting by the case, looking rather bored, I must admit!

A few "don'ts" about obedience:

Don't expect your dog to learn everything in a minute. Be patient.

Don't forget your pup is a "baby." Make your lessons short.

Don't tell your dog to do something unnecessary and harshly insist upon it. Dogs love justice.

Don't hit your dog because it does not understand. Explain again.

Don't forbid a thing one day and allow it the next. Inconsistency is a human privilege that is not understood by dogs.

Don't forget to praise your dog when it does the right thing.

The German Shepherd Dog is distinguished for its ability to assimilate and retain training for a number of special services.

The Dog In The Street

After a dog has been trained to obedience and cleanliness in the house, it is only half trained. A dog spends a great part of its life outside, and it must be educated in such a way that it is not a nuisance to other people or other dogs.

I have already spoken of cleanliness in the street and of the necessity of teaching a dog to use the gutter. Now I shall mention a few other points about street manners.

A pup must learn to walk beside its master and should be kept on the lead. This particularly applies in busy streets, but the pup may be loosed in a secluded area in order to teach it to walk close at hand.

Having arrived in a quiet area, remove the lead and continue the walk. Whenever the puppy begins to run ahead, call it back by saying: "Heel." If this is said, at first, in a warning voice the animal will usually slow down—not because it really understands but because it knows something is wrong.

If the puppy lags behind, as some do, it may be better to put it on the lead again for a few minutes. As a rule it is quite easy to teach dogs to keep close, and if they are never permitted to run on ahead while puppies they will probably never give any trouble when they grow up.

It is obvious, of course, that the dog must get a run sometimes, and it is therefore necessary to teach it when it may go for a run. A good way of doing this is to take a ball with you when you go out for a walk. Keep the dog on the lead until you reach an open space or field and then remove the lead. Show the ball to the dog, and throw it, saying: "Run!"

After a while the pup will understand that these words mean a game with the ball and, finally, that it means permission to run about. After trying several times with the ball, the phrase should be spoken when the field is reached, and as a rule the dog will understand.

Facing page: This German Shepherd Dog proudly displays his newly-won honor. Show enthusiasts maintain that nothing beats show competition for excitement—especially when your pet receives special recognition.

The sense of smell is a very important thing to a dog, and it sometimes means a little trouble for the owner. Dogs will stop to smell every few yards, and this will become a nuisance if not stopped. If the animal is allowed to run about in a field and sniff and smell to its heart's content, there is no need for it to smell every lamppost in the street. From the very beginning when the puppy stops to sniff, pull the lead gently but firmly. If this is done the dog will never contract the bad habit.

Another annoying habit that is common to dogs that are allowed to roam about loose is frequent urination. Dogs that only go out with their masters seldom do this, and the cure is obvious. Anyone who really likes a dog will find time to take it out when it requires to do so,

No matter what breed of dog you have or what training program you employ, your pet needs a special, comfy spot of its own.

Collie puppy. Arista Malashel's May Flower at ten weeks of age. Owner, Elaine Wishnow.

and also for a reasonable walk once a day. People who have yards, of course, find the matter simplified by allowing the dog the run of the yard. Dogs that run loose are no longer under the control of their masters and soon learn bad habits.

Fighting is another bad habit. Everyone wants a courageous dog and one that can stand up for itself if necessary, but a dog that is continually fighting is a positive nuisance. At the first signs of a quarrelsome spirit developing, the dog owner should speak sharply to his pet. Do not allow it to get into fights when it is young and it will not likely become a fighter when it grows. As for people who actually encourage their dogs to fight, I think they are unworthy of the guardianship of any animal.

Do not allow your dog to run after bicycles or motor cars. It might be the cause of a serious accident. No dog will learn this bad habit if it has been taught to follow properly and is not allowed to run free in the street. Should the animal already have the habit, the

Hip problems are less likely to develop in dogs that are exercised regularly.

At moments like this, a Poodle can hardly be blamed for barking in sheer delight. However, the habit of constant or senseless barking should be discouraged at an early age.

only cure is to reprove it sternly and always keep it on the lead.

It is always very important to teach your dog to keep to the sidewalk except when it must go to the gutter for a definite purpose. When the dog is on the lead, make a point of slowing down at the corners and saying: "Wait." When the crossing is clear, say: "Cross," and go over. This will be the beginning of traffic training, which is very useful to town dogs.

Whenever you remove the lead in a quiet street, keep careful watch. If the dog attempts to leave the pavement say: "Ach!" (or some other warning sound).

The dog will stop to see what is the matter. In a surprisingly short time the dog will understand that it must not leave the sidewalk. Never allow your dog to jump on people in the street. Muddy paws can be most annoying, and it is a habit that is easily prevented. Puppies should not be lifted and held in the lap, and never should they be allowed to put their paws on a stranger's legs. If this is done from the earliest puppyhood, the dog will never become a "jumper." Any attempt at jumping up should be sternly reproved.

Now a few "don'ts" about street manners:

Don't forget that the street is primarily for human beings. They have the first rights.

Don't forget that every time your dog annoys someone you are directly harming every dog owner.

Don't forget that streets have to be cleaned. Make your dog as clean as possible.

Don't forget that a carelessly trained dog may cause an accident and many deaths. Train your dog to keep to heel.

Don't encourage your dog to fight other dogs or to chase cats. There is no real fun in either. Dog fights and bull fights appeal to the same natures.

Some breeds of dog will make children the object of their care and concern.

Before you purchase a puppy, you should consider which dog breed suits your needs, your lifestyle, and your own temperament.

Pulling, Dragging, and Bolting

Pulling on the lead is one of the most common difficulties with dogs. Usually because the animal is happy and eager to get out, it will pull strongly on the lead, and to the dog's master this soon becomes tiring. It is rather difficult to teach an eager, healthy dog to walk quietly on the lead, without pulling, but it can be done with patience.

As soon as your dog begins to pull, speak to it in a soothing voice, saying: "Slooowly, slooowly," or a similar phrase. At the same time pull gently on the lead and hold it as short as possible. The shortening of the lead usually has the desired effect, for when the animal is kept close to your feet it seems to have less pulling power. The longer the lead the greater leverage there is for the dog's paws, and pulling will be accentuated. It is for this reason that experts keep large, powerful dogs on short leads.

If your dog persists in pulling, even after this treatment has been tried, something more drastic must be tried. I do not mean that the lead should be violently tugged. This is a useless practice and it may hurt the dog's throat if the lead is attached to a collar. There is a much more effective and less painful method.

On leaving the house, attach the lead to a choke collar around the dog's neck. Whenever the dog begins to pull, the collar should be slowly drawn tight. Although this is not enough to choke the dog, the tight collar causes a slight discomfort and the dog will usually ease up.

There is, however, positively no cruelty in this method, and, in fact, a dog is more likely to harm itself by constant pulling on the lead than by a little temporary "choking." I have cured a dog of seven years of age of the pulling habit by using this method, and the dog had been an inveterate "puller" all his life.

Facing page: A well-behaved Irish Setter. By the time your pet reaches adulthood, it should not resist such basic practices as having its collar put on.

When a dog is in the habit of dragging on the lead or pulling backwards, the same treatment may be used. This is by no means such a common fault as pulling, and is general only with puppies that are not yet accustomed to the lead. I have seen puppies dragged along the street until their haunches and hindlegs were raw flesh, and yet the little animal was unwilling to go quietly. This is absolutely unnecessary.

If you have a friend who has an older dog, go out with him and let your puppy see the other dog on the lead. This sometimes works, but I know of another method that never fails. Go again with your friend, and in a field put your puppy on the lead. Let your friend take the other end of the lead and with it play with his own dog.

Finally, allow the bigger dog to take the lead in its mouth, and in a minute or two the older dog will be running about with the puppy on the lead. If this is done a few times there should be no further difficulty with the puppy.

This girl is teaching her German Shepherd Dog puppy the command, "Come."

The Shih Tzu is an intelligent and even-tempered dog; its training should not be a difficult matter.

If none of these methods can be used, there is no other way but to put the lead on in the house, and play with the puppy. It will then speedily become accustomed to it.

Another bad habit is "bolting." Some dogs, the minute the door is opened, make a dash for "freedom," and there is always the risk of running into the middle of the street in the way of traffic.

Other dogs will bolt immediately when the lead is removed. This must not be allowed. The dog must wait until its master says: "Go," as I have already pointed out. Bolting must be cured while the dog is young.

The choke collar must this time be attached to a separate long cord. Before opening the door, or before removing the leash, as the case may be, place the collar around the dog's neck and coil the cord in your hand. When the dog bolts, allow the line to run until the dog is some yards away.

Then hold firmly and the collar will be drawn tight. This stops the dog and gives it a surprise. If the dog bolts again, the line should again be tightened, and so on until the dog gives up its bad habit.

I have found, as a rule, that puppies will stop bolting after this has been repeated some half-dozen times, perhaps three times one day, and three times the next. With older dogs it may take longer, but the result is always the same; finally the dog stops bolting.

Note with what grace and seeming ease this Collie jumps a hurdle.

I have found the long line and collar useful for pups that try to run back into the house before doing their "duty," and it is equally useful for teaching a dog not to run out of the yard every time the gate is opened. The method may require slight modification to suit each case, but I leave this to the intelligence of the reader.

A refrain of "don'ts:"

Don't allow your dog to pull. It hurts the dog's neck almost as much as your arm.

Don't tug the lead sharply; you may cause serious injury to your pet.

Don't allow your dog to drag. It looks silly and is silly.

Don't forget that a "bolting" dog may bolt under a car. Stop the bolting habit as soon as it appears.

Don't hang your dog when you use the choke collar. The collar should *draw* tight, not be *tugged* tight.

Facing page: This Labrador Retriever eagerly waits for his owner to toss his toy. The dense coat of the Lab is such that swimming in cooler weather does not make him uncomfortable.

Barking and Protecting

Barking may be a sign of warning, it may show pleasure or excitement, or it may be a confounded nuisance. A dog that barks when there is something to bark about is doing its duty or showing its feelings, but a dog that barks for the sake of barking is an irritation to everyone within hearing distance.

It will be noticed that pups never bark for nothing. There is always a reason for a pup's bark. But with grown dogs this is not always the case. Some dogs bark out of sheer bad habit. It is not natural in puppyhood and can therefore be prevented in the adult dog.

It is best to begin right with a puppy. When it barks at the right time, it should be praised, not scolded, for a dog that never barked would be useless as a watchdog. At the first sign of barking "for fun" the dog should be reproved. Speak sharply whenever the dog does it, and the chances are that the dog will never become a serious offender.

Of course, every dog will bark *apparently* for no reason at times, but the dog owner should use his intelligence in discovering whether the dog was right or not. A sudden,

sharp bark will usually have some reason behind it, and in this case there is no need for an immediate scolding. Speak assuringly, rather, and unless there is something seriously wrong the dog will usually settle down. If the barking should continue, however, the owner must try to find out what is the matter.

If, however, a dog sits in the yard and barks at everyone and everything in the street, it must be scolded. Speak sharply to the dog, saying: "Quiet!" and if the noise continues the dog should be removed to some other place.

When, for instance, there is a knock or a ring at your front door your dog will probably bark. This is very natural, for the dog thinks that your property is being threatened. However, it is most annoying for a perfectly harmless visitor to be greeted at the door by a barking, growling dog. It is obvious that it is usually harmless people who knock at your door; evil-doers seek a less obvious entrance. What to do with the barking dog, then? It thinks it is doing its duty and it must not be scolded.

As soon as the bell rings or the door is knocked upon and

If your dog has been trained to be a watchdog, it is wise to post an appropriate warning sign on your property.

the dog barks, say: "All right, Prince! Come and see!" Let the dog go to the door with you, speaking soothingly as you go. The dog will soon learn that people who come to the door are usually harmless, and at the same time you are providing for the unexpected by taking the dog with you.

If, by any strange chance, you should open the door and find a masked burglar, the dog will notice the difference. It will then bark to your complete satisfaction. Seriously, however, the dog will soon learn to distinguish between

Someone or something has aroused the curiosity of this Alaskan Malamute from Susan Kander's Suak Kennels.

Your finger should not be the object on which your puppy begins to teethe.

friends and foes when they appear at your front door. If it is a friend, on no account let your dog go on barking or growling. Pacify the animal with reassuring language, *and do not expect your friend to do the pacifying!*

Such absurd habits as barking at cars and cyclists must be nipped in the bud. Dogs get this habit for various reasons, but it must be

51

stopped as soon as it appears. Your dog will know when you are annoyed by the time it is three months old. If it barks at a cyclist or car, show your annoyance. If you do this from the very beginning your dog will never become a "yapper." In this, as in everything to do with dog training, the secret is to begin early and be consistent.

"This is all very well," says someone. "But I don't want a quiet, mannerly dog. I want a fierce, ferocious animal that will be able to defend me if necessary!"

I quite agree that a dog should be capable of defending its master within its power, but the dog need not be fierce or ferocious to do this. A ferocious dog is likely to do much more harm than good. The average dog will be quite prepared to fight for its master, although it may not fight for anything else, so very little is needed to make a dog a guard. A little encouragement may be useful, however.

For instance, while your dog is still young you may get a friend to help you. Ask your friend to threaten you with upraised arm. If this is not enough, let him hold your shoulder and shake you. There are plenty of friends who will be only too pleased to do this in a realistic manner. While this is being done, call your dog in an alarmed tone of voice, and encourage it to attack. Very little encouragement is, generally speaking, necessary.

One day I was out walking with a little mongrel puppy and a friend ran up behind me and took me by the arm. The puppy promptly bit his leg! True, this was excessive zeal on the puppy's part, but it is an example of your dog's protective spirit as far as its master is concerned.

What about our "don'ts?"

Don't ever let your dog bark at traffic.

Don't forget that your dog must bark sometimes. Dogs cannot speak English, but they can say a lot with a bark.

A Dalmatian in a stance of watchful attentiveness. Owner, Charlotte Katz.

Fetching and Staying

Although "fetching" may not be a really useful attainment in the ordinary household dog, many owners take pleasure in teaching their pets such things. There is absolutely no harm done in teaching a dog to fetch, and, in fact, anything that a dog may learn will serve to increase its intelligence. It may also happen at times that such an accomplishment may be decidedly useful.

I have always found that the best way of teaching a dog to fetch is by using a ball for play. Take your dog to a field and throw the ball until the dog is enjoying the fun. Then throw the ball a little further away and watch the dog run after it. When it has picked the ball up in its mouth, run backwards a few steps, and as a rule the dog will come running with the ball in its mouth. Repeat this several times, always saying: "Fetch" when the ball is thrown. It may take several tries before the dog understands what it has to do, but after a while it will not even be necessary for the owner to run backwards.

Some puppies, while still very young, will bring things to their master of their own free will. Such dogs will usually learn to be fine retrievers. After the dog has learned to fetch a ball, a stick should be used, and then some other object. This will teach it to fetch anything when the command is given.

Back-fetching is rather more difficult to teach. Its purpose is to teach the dog to go back and bring anything that its master may have dropped. The whole thing must be taught gradually in order to avoid boring the animal, but this really applies to all the phases of dog training.

If the dog has already learned to fetch a ball, take it with you when you go for a walk. When the dog is a little in front of you, drop the ball and walk on a few steps. Then stop, call the dog, and say: "Where's the ball?" Point to the ball and repeat the phrase. As soon as the dog sees the object, say: "Back-fetch," and

This German Shepherd Dog is waiting patiently for a command to drop the basket. Don't be discouraged if your pet fails in his efforts at first—all he probably needs is time and patience.

repeat it while the dog is running for it. Each time this is repeated, the distance should be a little greater; that is, you should walk a little further after dropping the ball before calling the dog.

When the animal has grasped the idea a glove or a stick should be used. If the

"trick" is taught gradually the dog will enjoy the fun and learn to go back a great distance looking for the lost object. My own dog will go back as much as a half-mile, turning various corners, to find anything I have dropped. It is a great advantage in this performance if the dog has a good nose, or if it has learned to use its nose. Some breeds of dog have a keener sense of smell than others, but all benefit by a little encouragement while the dog is young. Begin by showing the pup a bone and then put him out of the room. Trail the bone over the floor and hide it in some corner. Then let the pup in and start it where you began to trail the bone. The pup will follow the trail. Vary this exercise as much as you can.

"Stand-stay." Here a hand signal is being used to command the dog to remain in position while the trainer walks away.

Later get him to trail you outside. Go for a walk with your pup and a friend. While your friend holds the dog you should go and hide somewhere and then your friend can loose the dog and watch it trail you. This kind of game can be played in many ways and it encourages your dog to use its nose.

"Staying" can easily be taught as a supplement to back-fetching. Stop in the middle of your walk and make your dog sit down. Lay a glove at its feet, and holding up your finger say: "Stay!" Walk slowly away, repeating the command in a warning voice, and when you are a few yards away, call the dog. The dog will usually pick up the glove (or other object) the very first time, but in any case it will soon learn to do so.

Increase the distance every time, and never allow the dog to come before it is called. If it does so, take it back to the same place and repeat the command. This method has the additional advantage that the dog learns to guard an object, and for this reason vary the object as much as

Children should be taught to handle a pet gently and carefully.

Always respect your dog's wishes when it comes to nap time. A dog that is over-tired is not a good candidate for a training session.

possible. In time a dog will learn to sit and guard your property for as long as you like, and it is needless to emphasize the value of this.

Another form of staying that can be learned after this is staying and waiting outside shop doors, or any place where dogs are not admitted. Go right to the door, where the dog can see where you are going, and tell it to sit. Then say: "Stay," holding up your finger as you do so. Begin by going some place where you will not delay more than a few minutes and gradually extend the time.

I have already pointed out how a dog must learn to wait at corners, never crossing the street without permission. If this has been done since puppyhood, there should be no difficulty in teaching the other kinds of waiting.

There are many occasions in the daily life of a dog when the "staying" habit can be most useful, and no dog owner should miss teaching this to his pet.

Only one "don't" in this chapter.

Don't be in a hurry when teaching "fetching," "back-fetching" or "staying." Your dog will only learn when it understands. Have patience.

Teaching Your Dog Tricks

There is not very much to be said about this subject. Some people strongly object to teaching their dogs "tricks." They think that the dog is too dignified an animal to deserve such training. Personally, I see no harm in teaching a dog to beg, shake hands, play dead or any other accomplishment. Whatever dignity a dog may have, it is an inborn, natural thing that is in no way affected by these things. In any case, the basis of all these tricks is a natural act!

A stick, such as the one this Labrador Retriever holds in his mouth, may be dangerous to use as a playtoy.

For those who wish to teach their pets to perform tricks, this is a useful thing to remember. The dog naturally does certain things that can be transformed into "tricks" with a little patience.

For instance, most puppies beg naturally. When they are quite small they will beg for food without any teaching whatever. It is also true that most dogs forget this habit as they grow older, possibly because they find that they get food in any case. It is quite easy, however, to encourage your dog to keep up the habit. While he is still a puppy always say: "Beg" when he does beg, and he will never forget how to do it when told.

If you have an older dog and have never seen him beg, encourage him to do so by offering him a tidbit, which should be held over his nose when he is sitting. As he raises his mouth to take it, raise your

Facing page: Sprightly leaps are natural for the Poodle, with its lively, energetic nature. Owner, Joy Grouf, Dancer Poodles.

hand slightly. In time he will beg properly, just as he could do when he was a little puppy. Some breeds do not seem to beg naturally. I bred Dachshunds for some time, but never saw a puppy beg. Possibly the dog's long body and short legs made this difficult, although I've seen other long-bodied dogs beg perfectly.

Any time you see your dog do anything unusual, give it a name. If your dog stretches himself by laying his forelegs along the floor with his other end in the air (as dogs often do), say to him: "Salaam" or "Great is Allah!" or something else which sounds suitable. The dog will soon learn to repeat the action when the name is mentioned.

One of my own dogs had the habit of sitting down and raising one paw instead of begging. I called this saluting,

Gumadisc®, the flying disc with the bone on top, is a great product to have on hand when teaching your dog retrieving tricks. It is available at your local pet shop.

"Shake hands." With the dog in the "Sit" position, push against his right shoulder with your left hand. As his foot comes up, take it in your right hand and shake it as you say "Shake hands."

and the dog learned to salute when commanded. It is little natural acts of this kind which are developed into "tricks." Anyone can do it who has the patience and wish.

Just one "don't" about tricks. Tricks are not very important. *Don't,* therefore, annoy your dog by insisting on teaching him tricks that don't interest him.

Obedience Trial Competition

Once you begin training your dog and see how well he does, you'll probably be bitten by the "obedience bug." If you own a purebred dog, you may be eligible to enter him in obedience trials held under the auspices of your national kennel club. If not, there are informal "match" trials in which all dogs can compete for ribbons and inexpensive trophies. These shows are run by many local clubs and all-breed obedience clubs. In many localities the humane society and other groups conduct their own obedience shows. Your local newspaper, pet shop proprietor or kennel club can keep you informed as to the location of shows in your vicinity.

Whether competing at official obedience trials or informal matches, there are several basic commands that form the basis of obedience competition. As your dog masters the commands, more

As part of his police dog training program, this German Shepherd Dog is learning to scale a nine-foot wall.

This Collie is executing a broad jump. The breed category of the qualifying dog determines the length of the jump.

and more will be expected of him. A.K.C. trials are divided into three classes based on the expertise of the dog: Novice, Open and Utility.

Obedience trial competition involves a great amount of work for both the handler and dog. You should never begin *serious* obedience training before your dog is seven or eight months old and has learned to walk nicely on a lead and come when he is called. If your dog shows an aptitude and interest for learning, you can proceed to teach him the basic commands that are required of obedience trial competitors.

A man and his dog. This Giant Schnauzer enjoys a well-bonded friendship with his master. Such companionship comes about as a result of treating the dog with affection and patience, whether training him to "Heel" or taking him through the rugged paces of field trials.

Welsh Springer Spaniels (top left), a mixed breed (top right), a Beagle (middle left), Basset Hounds (middle right), and the West Highland Terrier (right) represent different temperaments. Tailor your dog's training program to suit his individuality.

If you are planning a show career for your purebred dog, be aware that he must be on his best behavior at all times when in the judging ring. Not only must the dog be completely obedient, he must be a willing competitor that takes pride in himself and tries to please his master by performing as instructed. The fixed stance for examination and the graceful movements around the show ring exhibited by experienced competitors are carefully prepared techniques aimed at presenting the dog at his very best before the eyes of the judge.

Competition for the points that lead to a championship title (the quest of all dog show competitors) is especially keen, and the way the dog is presented is often a determining factor in the judge's decision. Practice in exhibiting technique should be perfected before the dog ever steps into the show ring. This is out of courtesy for the judge and other competitors that have already learned the skill of proper handling and exhibiting. A dog that is unruly or overly awkward in the ring, no matter how fine a specimen

he is, is not being shown to his best advantage and cannot be properly evaluated by the judge. Training and drilling for show competition should be practiced at home for at least several months prior to the start of a show career.

THE STAND FOR EXAMINATION

The primary basis for the judge's evaluation of the quality of a dog is from going over the dog's body to determine its soundness and how well it conforms to the mandates of the breed standard of perfection. It is of primary importance that you know the proper show stance that is expected for your breed. Ask a knowledgeable fancier or breeder to show you how to properly *stack* (that is, to stand in a show pose) your dog. Once you know the proper positioning, you can begin to accustom your dog to standing and holding the proper pose.

Facing page: Lhasa Apsos are spunky little characters capable of learning a variety of tricks. This adult Lhasa and its pups are owned by Terre Mohr.

The mixed breed pup (top left), Cardigan Welsh Corgi (top right), Norwich Terrier (middle left), Blenheim Spaniel (middle right), and Bearded Collie (left) are alert and eager learners.

The Great Pyrenees Mountain Dog (right) and the Smooth Fox Terrier (below) represent two distinctly different groups of dogs; the Working Group and the Terrier Group. Both share in common, however, the ability to learn many commands.

Once your dog walks easily on lead and will remain quietly by your side, you can begin working on the stand. Command the dog to "stay," and gently but firmly pull up on the lead to force the head up. Retain this grip throughout the initial steps, as it will help keep the dog still. Of course, be sure you are not choking the dog in any way. Carefully reach down with the free hand and lift the dog's leg into position one foot at a time. When all four feet are properly set, slacken up a bit on the lead to allow the head to lower to proper position. If the dog should make any attempt at moving throughout the entire process, command him to stay and correct him strongly if he starts to move. As he progresses and becomes more cooperative at standing, try moving a few feet in front of him at the end of the lead. Reprove him if he should move and return him to the proper position.

A pair of Lhasa Apsos. Pictured are Champion Karma Dmar-Pos and Karma Karha-Ta, photographed as puppies. Owner, Dorothy Cohen.

If you plan a show career for your dog, keep him accustomed to being with people and being handled by people.

Once he is fairly proficient at standing, it is time to introduce the hardest element of this exercise: standing while a stranger runs his hands over his body and legs. The dog must remain calm and hold his position steadfastly. At first he will balk at the approach of the stranger, but reassure him and stand by his side during the inspection. If he should move, immediately return him to position. Only when the dog accepts this type of inspection can you allow your surrogate judge to try to examine the mouth to see if the dog has the proper bite. Needless to say, if the dog is not under control the result of such an inspection could be disastrous. It is best for the owner to lift the lips to expose the bite, at least until the dog is totally comfortable with the examination.

GAITING AND MOVING THE DOG

During the course of the evaluation by the judge, he will ask the handlers several times

Above: Though this Labrador Retriever is satisfying his urge to chew, the object of his attention is not safe for this purpose. **Facing page:** The Border Terrier (top left), the Bearded Collie (top right), and the Wirehaired Fox Terrier pups (bottom) will respond, like all dogs, to kind and patient treatment.

to move their dogs around the ring. By watching the dogs move as a group and alone, the judge evaluates whether or not the dogs move in the prescribed manner for that breed. Among the most common faults of dogs is not having the correct pattern of movement, which generally signifies that the legs or hips are not set or formed properly.

Each breed is expected to move in a certain manner and the official breed standard will generally describe the desired overall gait. However, knowing how to move the dog in certain patterns will serve to present the dog at his best. Once in the show ring, the judge will ask the entire group of competitors to move about the ring in one direction, then in the opposite. After examining each dog, he will generally ask the handlers to move the dogs out once more, this time individually. The judge will tell you exactly in which pattern he would like you to run your dog, and there are several patterns that he can choose from. For a complete explanation of particular gaiting patterns and

how to show your dog to his best advantage, please refer to T.F.H.'s *How to Show Your Own Dog,* by Virginia Tuck Nichols, which finely details this procedure.

The main point to remember when moving your dog is that *you* do not want to interfere with *his* best gait. It is important that the dog be accustomed to moving freely, not having to be tugged along by the lead. One of the most common mistakes of the novice handler is restraining and moving the dog too slowly, for the dog cannot move naturally if his handler is not giving him the opportunity to reach out and take normal strides. In practicing for this exercise, remember that the judge wants to see a dog that moves with a lively step and proudly holds his head up high. You should gait him on a loose lead and should not have to choke him to keep his head up. Practicing this exercise should be a fun routine for you and your dog, as it provides exercise and experience for the show career ahead.

This Golden Retriever is about to enjoy its Nylabone®, a product designed as a therapeutic device to vent doggie frustration. Owner, Nancy Strouss.

Looking bright and alert are two varieties of Dachshunds: the Wirehaired variety (above) and the Longhaired Variety (left). Brightness in a dog is an indication that he can be easy to train.

The Dachshund's history in field work goes back a long time, to the days when the breed was used to hunt game right down into underground burrows. This is the reason that the elongated, short bodies were bred for.

Having started to train your dog—and found that it is not really as difficult as you thought—there is something else that is very important.

It is not much use having a well-trained dog if it is not feeling very well. In fact, if a dog is not feeling well, it may be very difficult to train him at all. "Happy, healthy and wise" applies to dogs just as much as to human beings.

There are a number of diseases of an infectious nature which can be fatal to your dog. Among these I would list distemper, hard-pad, hepatitis, leptospirosis, and rabies.

Distemper is an illness caused by a virus. Once the illness is present, it is extremely difficult to cure, in spite of all the advances in medical science. Wonder drugs or not, viral diseases are sometimes fatal. Hard-pad is a type of distemper which unfortunately tends to affect the brain, spine or nervous system. It is difficult to treat. Hepatitis is an infectious disease which may affect the liver, the blood vessels, the brain and kidneys. It is, perhaps, neither as common nor as frequent as the two previously mentioned diseases but still kills many dogs (particularly young ones) every year. Leptospirosis actually refers to two types of infection. One can cause chronic illness and shortness of life; the other can be acute and kill within hours. Leptospirosis can affect human beings, as distinct from the diseases described before.

What can be done about these illnesses? Once an animal has contracted one or more of these troubles, it is unlikely that anyone but a fully-qualified veterinarian can do much to help. And it must be said that in spite of medical progress and new drugs, a very large percentage of animals never fully recover, and many die. Possibly, if a dog was seen very soon after being infected, a veterinarian could make it well. But it must be remembered that with many of these diseases the dog shows little or no obvious signs of illness and the owner might well think it is just "out of sorts." Many dogs infected with distemper show no

Facing page: Proper diet and care are essential elements for your dog's good health. These pointers are owned by Michael Zollo.

This Cocker Spaniel and its feline companion illustrate the fact that dogs and cats are not "natural enemies." A puppy and a kitten that are raised together can become good friends.

noticeable symptoms of illness until they begin to have convulsions or cry all night. It must also be remembered that once a dog (especially a young one) has contracted one of these diseases, he may also be susceptible to infection from a number of other diseases. In these circumstances the animal's chance of survival is minimal.

Hepatitis can pose serious problems for canines. Unfortunately, it can be life-threatening in puppies and may even account for the death of every pup in a litter. It is a disease which may be carried by adult dogs and still

Dogs enjoy a good hearty yawn just as much as people do.

These Irish Setters can safely enjoy playing outdoors because they have been confined to a fenced-in area.

This Cocker Spaniel (left), this Miniature Schnauzer (below), and these Shetland Sheepdogs (facing page), are all well-behaved. Their composure represents careful training by patient, dedicated owners.

kill puppies.

One type of leptospirosis can infect a dog while it is still very young and possibly show very little signs of illness at the time. The young animal might be out of sorts for a day or two and then seems to be perfectly back to normal. The problem is that the dog, when it reaches the age of six or seven years, shows signs of chronic kidney trouble. Degeneration of the kidneys can be treated up to a point, but the animal's life is certainly going to be shortened. The other type of leptospirosis causes much more acute problems. The dog may vomit blood and have dysentery. It can die in a matter of hours. The bacteria of this infectious disease are prevalent in rodents, especially rats. Consequently, dogs living near any possible source of rat contamination are running a severe risk.

Don't wait until your pet becomes sick before you seek the services of a veterinarian. The best prevention for the diseases that have been discussed is immunization with annual vaccination.

This little Pomeranian is learning the "Stay" command.

The Pembroke Welsh Corgi (left), originally trained as a cattle herder and hunting dog, has the capacity for learning other commands well. The German Shorthaired Pointer (below), represents field-working excellence. **Facing page:** The Silky Terrier is depicted at rest in a field after a training session.

The majestic-looking Collie is a responsive, active dog that is quite capable of being trained.

Index

Overleaf: *Always remember to praise your pet when it obeys your commands.*

BASIC DOG TRAINING
KW-022